The New Small Temples of The Church of Jesus Christ of Latter-day Saints

Counted Cross-stitch Patterns For Current and Future Small Temples

Designed by

Jean D. Crowther

The patterns and instructions in this book were designed, tested and proofread carefully. However, mistakes in printing or individual stitching challenges occasionally occur. We apologize for any inconvenience.

ISBN: 0-88290-682-8

Published by
Horizon Publishers
A division of Cedar Fort Inc.
www.cedarfort.com

Printed and distributed
in the United States of America by

CEDAR FORT

Mailing Address:
925 North Main Street
Springville, Utah 84663

Local Phone: (801) 489-4084
Toll Free: 1 (800) SKYBOOK
FAX: (800)489-1097

E-mail: skybook@cedarfort.com
www.cedarfort.com

Contents

Introduction

Members of The Church of Jesus Christ of Latter-day Saints have been counseled to display pictures of the temples in their homes to remind themselves and their families of their eternal goal of exaltation together. This book of temple patterns has been designed and charted for counted cross stitching to help members follow this counsel and to assist them in beautifying their surroundings.

Temple building took on an exciting new emphasis in 1997 when President Gordon B. Hinckley announced the concept of small temples to the Church. Horizon Publishers and Distributors, Inc., has endeavored, over the years, to provide Church members with individual patterns of each new temple as the temple has been completed. However, with many temples being built to the same design, a new approach was needed.

Since the exterior design of these small temples is very similar, I have chosen to provide three patterns of specific temples with an effort to show views from different angles. I have then included the variations of stone colors, Angel Moroni's direction, and landscaping details, etc. Directions are included on how to use these variations to customize the particular temple being stitched. It is hoped that this approach to designing will furnish the stitcher with the ability to create a unique pattern for the individual temple desired.

Over the years, I have heard from hundreds of people who have indicated the enjoyment that these temple patterns have provided them. They have stitched lovely pieces of art for themselves and to be shared with their families and friends. May all the recipients draw strength and inspiration for everyday living from having this stitchery in their homes, and may we all be blessed by the guidance, instruction and inspiration received in the sacred temples.

Jean D. Crowther

About the Author

Jean D. Crowther has combined her knowledge of the writer's art and her needlework to provide cross-stitch patterns for the temples of The Church of Jesus Christ of Latter-day Saints and other religious symbols and pictures. Thousands of stitched replicas of her designs hang in homes, chapels, seminaries and other edifices worldwide. Her temple patterns are published in 9 New Mormon Temples, 10 New Mormon Temples, 11 More New Mormon Temples,13 New Mormon Temples, 14 New Mormon Temples, New Small Temples, The Utah Temples and in numerous leaflets and individual downloadable formats. She has adapted the famous drawings of the well-known Christian artists Frances and Richard Hook in Jesus and the Children, A Savior is Born, Prayer, Jesus of Nazareth, and crafted an adaptation of da Vinci's The Last Supper. In addition, she served as needle-craft editor for Horizon Publishers in creating 28 cross-stitch books from colored pencil graphs submitted by other designers as well as producing other cross-stitch books of her own: Pedigree Patterns, Especially for Primary, Especially for Young Women, Especially for Women, Murphy Strikes Again, Country Life, Country Wisdom, Darling Dinosaurs and Puppies and Pooches. She is also the author of other books including The Joy of Being a Woman, What Do I Do Now, Mom?, How To Get Married and Survive It, A Mother's Prayer, Book of Mormon Puzzles and Pictures, Growing Up a Mormon and The Very First Christmas.

Jean lives in Bountiful, Utah with her husband, Duane S. Crowther, a noted author. They are the parents of a fine family of four sons, four daughters, four daughters-in-law and three sons-in-law. They currently have thirty-five precious grandchildren and twenty-three great-grandchildren with more on their way.

A List of Temples to Be Stitched from These Patterns

Between 1999 and 2005, The Church of Jesus Christ of Latter-day Saints built 42 temples throughout the world based on the same basic exterior design. These temples face different directions so the Angel Moroni, which always faces east, often looks different on each temple. Rather than creating many different but nearly identical patterns, we designed three different views, and looking at based on specific temples: The Spokane Washington (the front entrance), The Columbia South Carolina (the Celestial room side), and The Palmyra New York (from the left side). Stitchers are invited to choose one of these three views and then use pages 22-24 for instructions on how to vary the stone colors, the landscaping details, and the direction that the Angel Moroni faces to individualize the designs. Photos of each temple can also be found on the Church website and the internet which will be helpful.

A. The following 35 temples can be stitched using these three designs:

Aba Nigeria Temple
Adelaide Australia Temple
Birmingham Alabama Temple
Bismarck North Dakota Temple
Brisbane Australia Temple
Ciudad Juarez México Temple
Columbia South Carolina Temple
Detroit Michigan Temple
Edmonton Alberta Temple
Fresno California Temple
Fukuoka Japan Temple
Guadalajara México Temple
Halifax Nova Scotia Temple
Hermosillo Sonora México Temple
Kona Hawaii Temple
Louisville Kentucky Temple
Medford Oregon Temple
Melbourne Australia Temple
Mérida Yucatán México Temple
Montevideo Uruguay Temple
Nashville Tennessee Temple
Oaxaca México Temple
Palmyra New York Temple
Perth Australia Temple
Pôrto Alegre Brazil Temple
Regina Saskatchewan Temple
Reno Nevada Temple
San José Costa Rica Temple
Spokane Washington Temple
St. Paul Minnesota Temple
Suva Fiji Temple
Tampico México Temple
Tuxtla Gutiérrez México Temple
Veracruz México Temple
Villahermosa Tabasco México Temple

B. Four temples have been renovated with changes made to the entrances, towers and windows. The Raleigh North Carolina Temple, the Baton Rouge Louisiana, the Columbus Ohio and the Memphis Tennessee temples can be stitched to the Raleigh Temple design on pages 16-17, after changing the direction of the Angel Moroni, the stone colors and the landscape details.

C. The Oklahoma City Oklahoma Temple and the Asunción Paraguay Temple were built to the original design that was flip-flopped 180°, so a specific design for them is included in this book on pages 20-21.

D. Completely different designs were used for the Monticello Utah Temple, the Anchorage Alaska Temple, and the Colonia Juarez Chihuahua Temple. They are found on pages 9–11.

General Instructions

A Helpful Hint for Beginning—After locating the center of the chart and the material, count to the nearest window or vertical shaded area and stitch that first. Continue in the same direction, stitching the vertical windows and shaded areas to the outer right edge of the temple, skipping the main temple color. Return to the center and work the same areas to the left edge of the temple. The main colors of the temple will be easy to fill in after the detail work is completed. This approach will reduce the possibility of counting errors because the squares to be counted are fewer.

Basic Cross-stitch Technique—Form the habit of always stitching in the same direction. This helps your work to have a smooth, uniform appearance. All first diagonals should be stitched in the same direction (see *Figure 1*). Using a hoop to stretch the cloth will help keep the stitches uniform in tension.

Half Stitches—In some areas, the graph may show a smaller symbol in one section of a square. To create this partial stitch, work from the corner hole to the center of the square, placing the needle between the threads (see *Figure 2*). Complete the square with a half-stitch across the other angle (or the backstitch outline color where designated). Occasionally, a vertical or horizontal half-stitch will be indicated. These should be stitched with a very shallow v-stitch, crossing from each of the two corner holes to the center of the square (see *Figure 3*). *Note:* In many areas of a pattern the horizontal backstitch outline covers the symbol so two smaller duplicate symbols have been placed within the square. These are for clarification only and should be worked as a single cross stitch.

Backstitch Outlining—The backstitching generally should be done after all the cross stitching is complete. Anchor the thread and bring the needle up in an appropriate place in the pattern. Place the needle down in the hole behind the initial stitch. Continue working one stitch-length back on top of the fabric, and two stitch-lengths forward beneath the fabric, to form a solid line (see *Figure 4*). To create a gentler angle, sometimes a single backstitch will travel more than two or three squares vertically or horizontally (see *Figure 5*). Care must be taken with these longer stitches to keep the floss tension even.

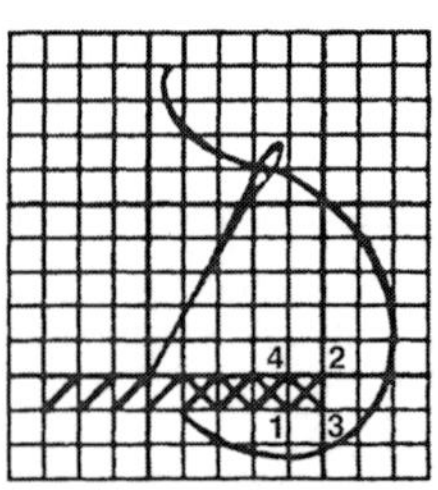

Figure 1
Basic Cross-stitch

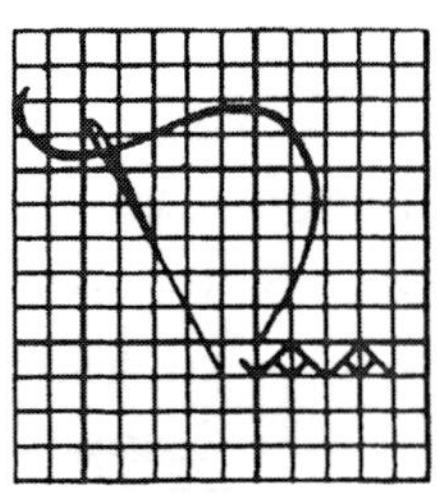

Figure 2
Half Stitch

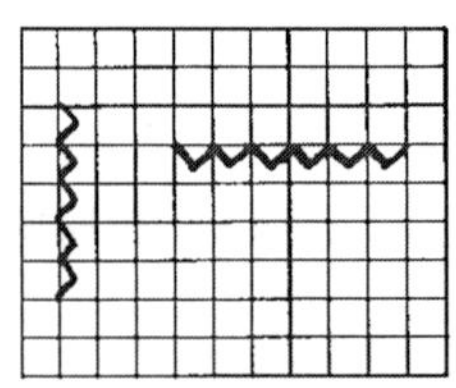

Figure 3
Horizontal or Vertical Half Stitch

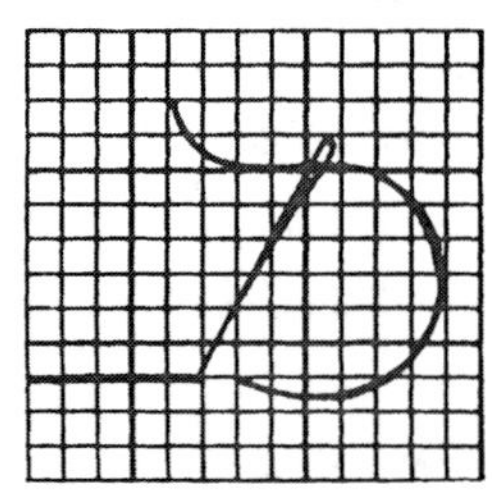

Figure 4
Backstitch Outline

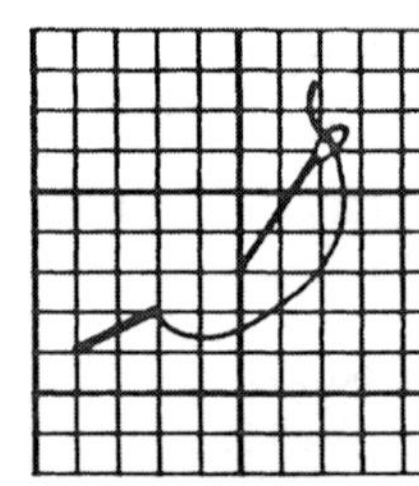

Figure 5
Over-two Backstitch

Slanted Roof Lines and Spires—Most temples in this book have roof lines or spires slanted at different angles than is possible to indicate with even the "over-three" stitch. In order to create a relatively accurate angle, a longer line is needed. Study the individual squares of Aida cloth and observe that the material is woven with four threads vertically and crossed with four threads horizontally within the square (see *Figure 6.*) This creates five places between threads that the needle can enter the cloth and keep the backstitches evenly placed as the line is created (see *Figure 7*). Since it is best to use stitches not more than three squares long, count out the complete length of the backstitch roof or tower line and divide by two or three. This total calculates how many backstitches will be needed for the complete line. Make sure that the thread enters exactly the same exit point between the threads used by the previous stitch in order to create a straight line.

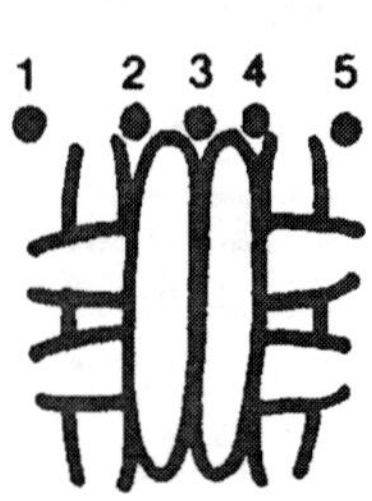

Figure 6
Openings Between Threads

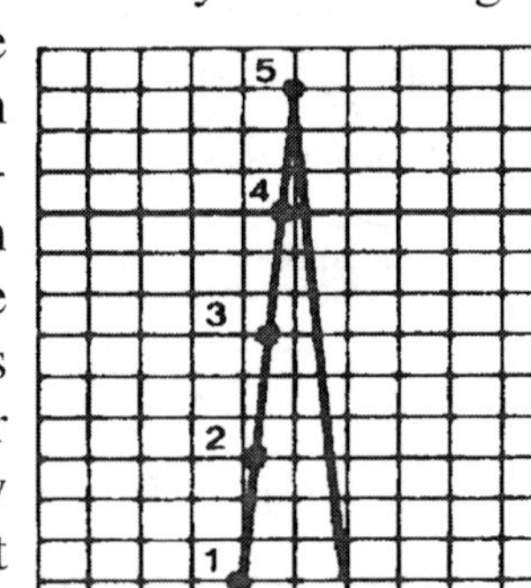

Figure 7
Needle Entry Points

Fill-in Partial Stitches—When working cross stitches to fill in the squares of the areas created by longer backstitch lines, it is necessary to make a different-angled stitch. It is easier to leave the partial-stitch areas blank until after backstitching. Then carefully create partial stitches, making sure to stay inside the backstitches as your needle enters the material. To fill in next to an "over-two" backstitch, begin at the corner hole of the narrowest square and make a very shallow-angled half stitch. The adjoining square can be filled in with a standard half stitch (see *Figure 8*). Longer areas should be done in the same manner, increasing the angles as needed (see *Figures 9* and *10*). When two different colors meet, it is necessary to use the same fill-in techniques for both colors (see *Figure 11*).

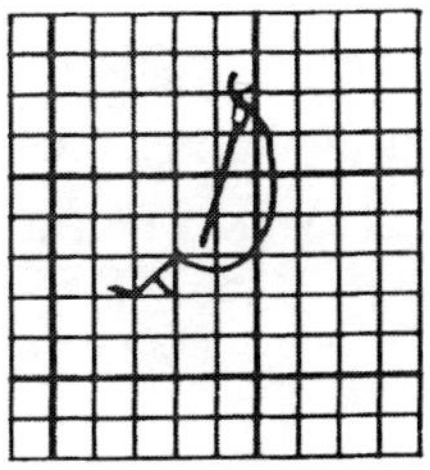

Figure 8
Over-two Fill-in Stitch

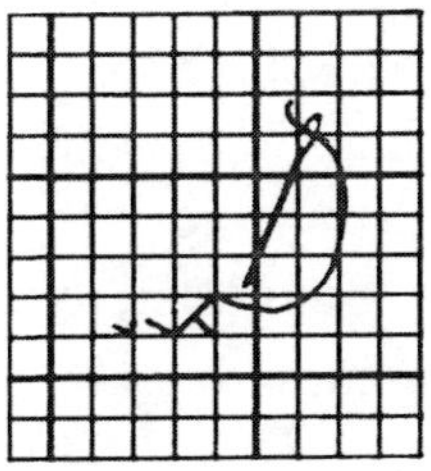

Figure 9
Over-three Fill-in Stitch

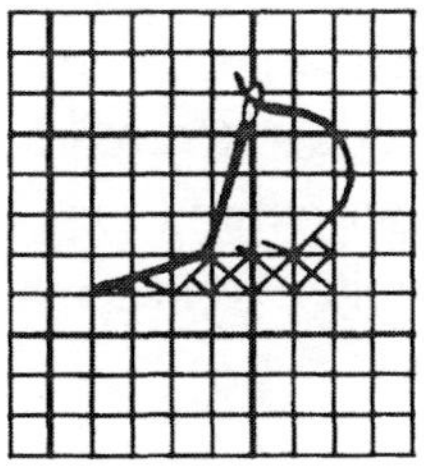

Figure 10
Fill-in Stitches with Over-three Backstitch

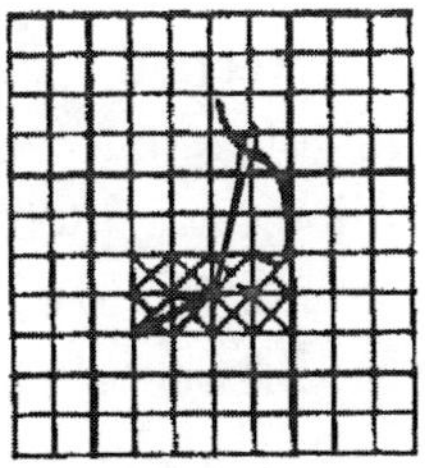

Figure 11
Fill-in Two Colors Meeting with Over-two Backstitch

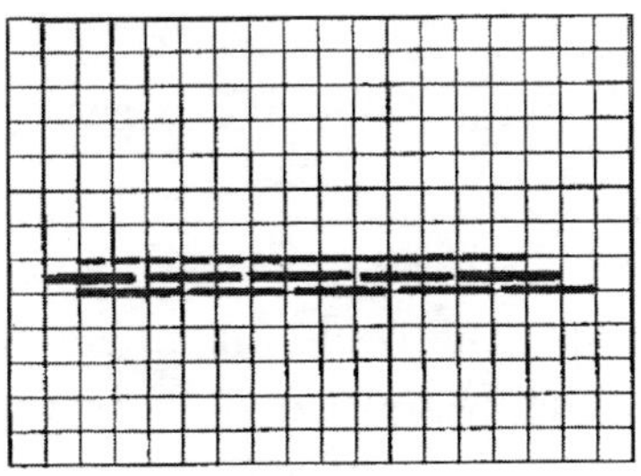

Figure 12
Perle Coton and Floss Ledge Backstitch

Backstitches of Horizontal Ledges—To indicate the architectural detail of horizontal ledges, a technique of using different amounts of floss or *Perle Coton* has been designed. These horizontal areas have been usually left blank on the charts since the heavier thread will cover the areas. If you desire more three-dimensional ledges, leave these areas without stitching until the rest of the temple is completed. To create the ledges, First: stitch across the top of the squares with two strands of the basic backstitching color as indicated. Second: stitch across the bottom of the squares with 2-3 strands of white floss, as indicated, stitching over three squares at a time. Third: use one strand of #5 *Perle Coton* down the middle of the squares, stitching over three squares at a time. Make sure that the breaks in the corresponding floss line underneath the *Perle Coton* are offset so the ends and beginnings of each stitch are not as obvious (see *Figure 12*). A larger tapestry needle will be needed for the Perle Coton.

Backstitches Down the Middle of the Square—Some details are indicated by backstitching down the center of the squares over the background color. Be careful to keep this line straight by finding the center hole (#3 on *Figure 6*) with every stitch. If these areas are on the edge of the pattern, the fill-in stitch will be made diagonally from the middle of the square to a corner hole (see *Figure 13*).

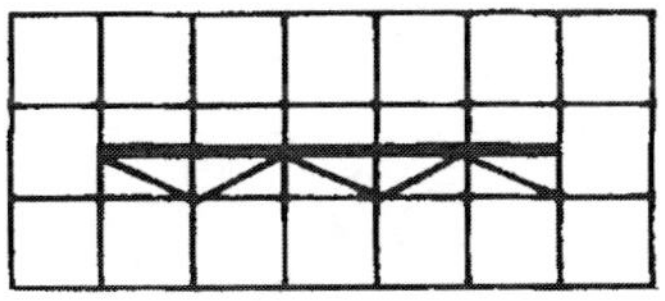

Figure 13
Fill-in Stitches with the Middle of Square Backstitch

Angel Moroni—The angel on top of the temple is indicated in the charts by the regular backstitch line surrounded by a dashed line. **Do not stitch the dashed line around the angel on each temple. It is there to indicate the difference between the gold floss backstitching and the regular backstitch color.** To create a metallic gold appearance, the angel can be worked with gold floss combined with metallic floss or blending filament. A metallic floss, divisible into six strands and very easy to use, is available from both DMC and Anchor. It is suggested that the stitcher begins with two strands of gold floss and one strand of metallic floss in the needle. The ratio of floss to metallic thread can be changed as desired. *Note:* the angel's head and the ball he stands upon are indicated by an asterisk (*). This is worked either in the center of the square or between two squares by first working a normal cross stitch (x) and then a (+) directly on top of the (x), thus creating the round (*). The rest of the angel is finished in a regular backstitch.

Inscription Lines—On some temples, the "House of the Lord" inscription is visible and indicated by short horizontal backstitch lines. They should be stitched, if applicable, with two strands of gold floss and, if desired, one strand of metallic floss or blending filament.

Material Needed—The design size (the number of squares covered by the actual design) is given on each chart. The finished size of the temple will be determined by the count of the even weave fabric used. It can be calculated by dividing the two design-size numbers by the number of squares per inch of the material chosen. After determining that measurement, add at least two inches to all four sides of the design to allow adequate material for finishing or framing.

Floss Needed—The general rule is to use one less strand for backstitching than was used for cross stitching. However, more strands may be added to create more distinct lines in the lettering, the window frames and the outline backstitching. The stitcher should experiment in order to achieve the desired effect. When using extra strands of floss, care must be taken to keep the tension even. Suggested amounts are:

Material Count	*Cross-Stitches*	*Backstitching*
11-count Aida	3 strands	2-4 strands
14-or 16-count Aida	2 strands	1-3 strands
18-count Aida, 22-count Hardanger and Linen worked over two squares	1-2 strands	1-2 strands

In this book, the color numbers are given for the three major brands of floss which are generally available: embroidery floss from *The DMC Corporation* of Elizabeth, NJ; *Anchor* floss, made by *Susan Bates* of Chester, CT, and *Wound Embroidery Floss* manufactured by *J. & P. Coats* of Jacksonville, FL. Because of the individual color differences and variations in light-reflection characteristics, the floss from the different companies should not be mixed in a single stitchery design.

Finishing Instructions—Always stitch with clean hands. Even if your completed stitchery doesn't appear soiled, it is best to hand-wash it with mild soap and warm water when finished, just as you would fine lingerie. Rinse the article carefully and blot it with a clean bath towel without wringing, folding, or squeezing the material. Place the wet stitchery, floss-side down, on a dry bath towel, making sure the fabric isn't twisted. Iron until completely dry and the background cloth looks smooth, with the embroidery and background lines straight. In areas where metallic threads are used, a pressing cloth might be needed. Handle the project carefully until it is permanently mounted.

Monticello Utah Temple Chart and Instructions

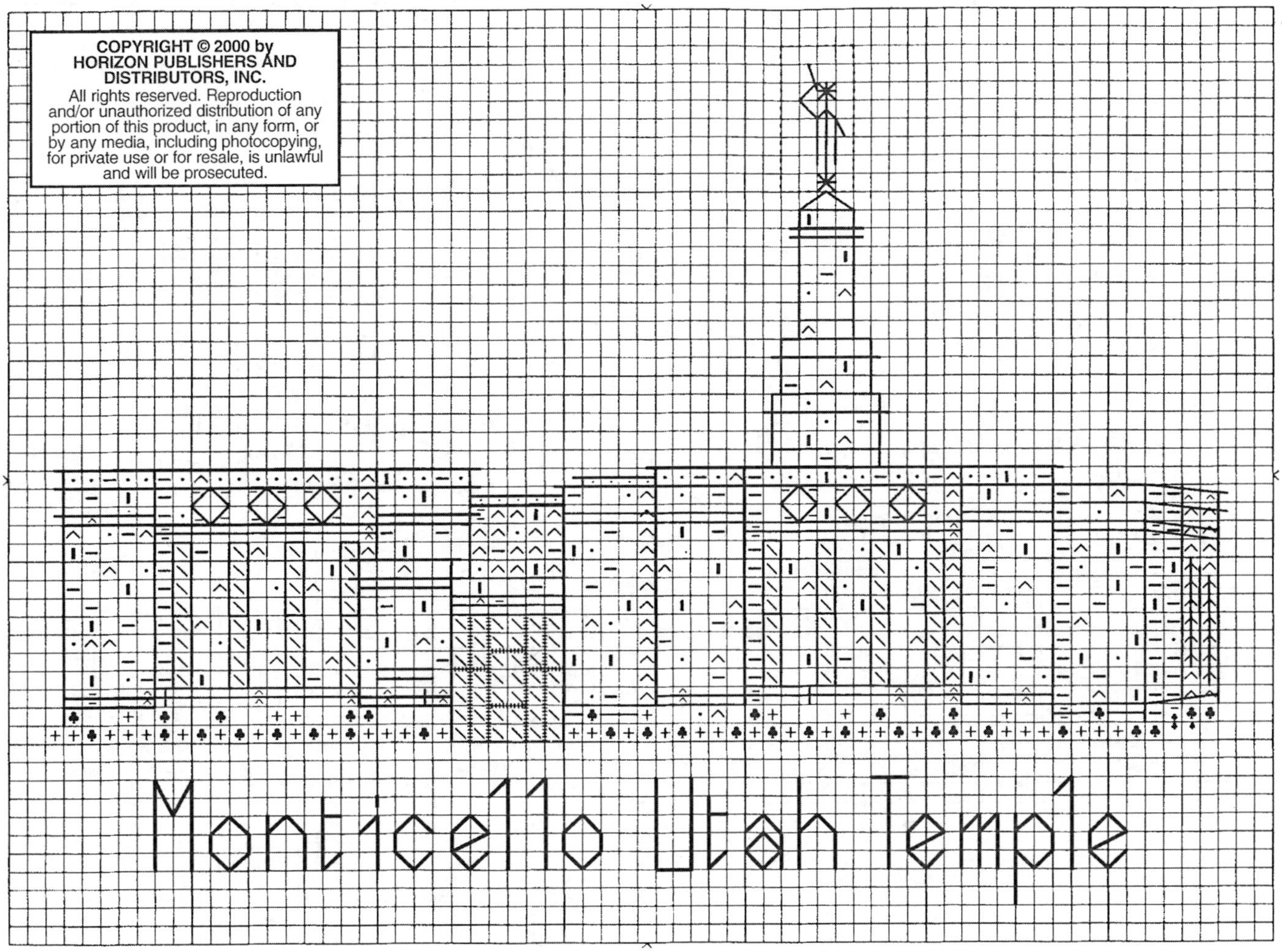

Design size: 61 x 37 squares; 61 x 46 with name of temple included.

Symbol	DMC	Anchor	JP Coats	Color Name	Description
☐ (within pattern)	712	926	2275	cream	main body of temple
•	ecru	387	5387	off-white	varied stone color
—	3864	376	5576	pale cocoa	light shadowing and stone variations
^	3863	6	3146	light cocoa	medium shadowing and stone variations
I	543	933	5533	beige	varied stone color
\	775	128	7031	light blue	windows and glass door
+	989	242	6266	light green	shrubs
♣	987	244	6258	medium green	shrubs
'''''''''''	ecru	926	2275	off-white	backstitch in front door area
———	632	936	5936	light brown	backstitch outline of temple
———	3820	307	2307	gold	backstitch Angel Moroni (within dashed lines)

Special Instructions:

Although the general color of this temple is a pinkish cream, the stone of this temple has color striations spread through it. If you wish to indicate this marbling, stitch the main color and shadings of the temple first. Then, using just one strand of varied light colors as indicated in the above table and as suggested in the chart, randomly stitch a full cross-stitch or the first diagonal stitch on top of the existing stitches.

Before beginning to stitch this temple, be sure to read the *General Instructions* on pages 5-7 for information on partial stitches, the ledges, and the Angel Moroni.

DO NOT STITCH the dashed lines around the Angel Moroni. They are there to indicate that the angel and ball are to be backstitched with gold floss. The gold floss can be combined with a metallic floss or blending filament, if desired, to add a gold shine to the project.

This temple is located in Monticello Utah. It was dedicated July 26, 1998.

Anchorage Alaska Temple Chart and Instructions

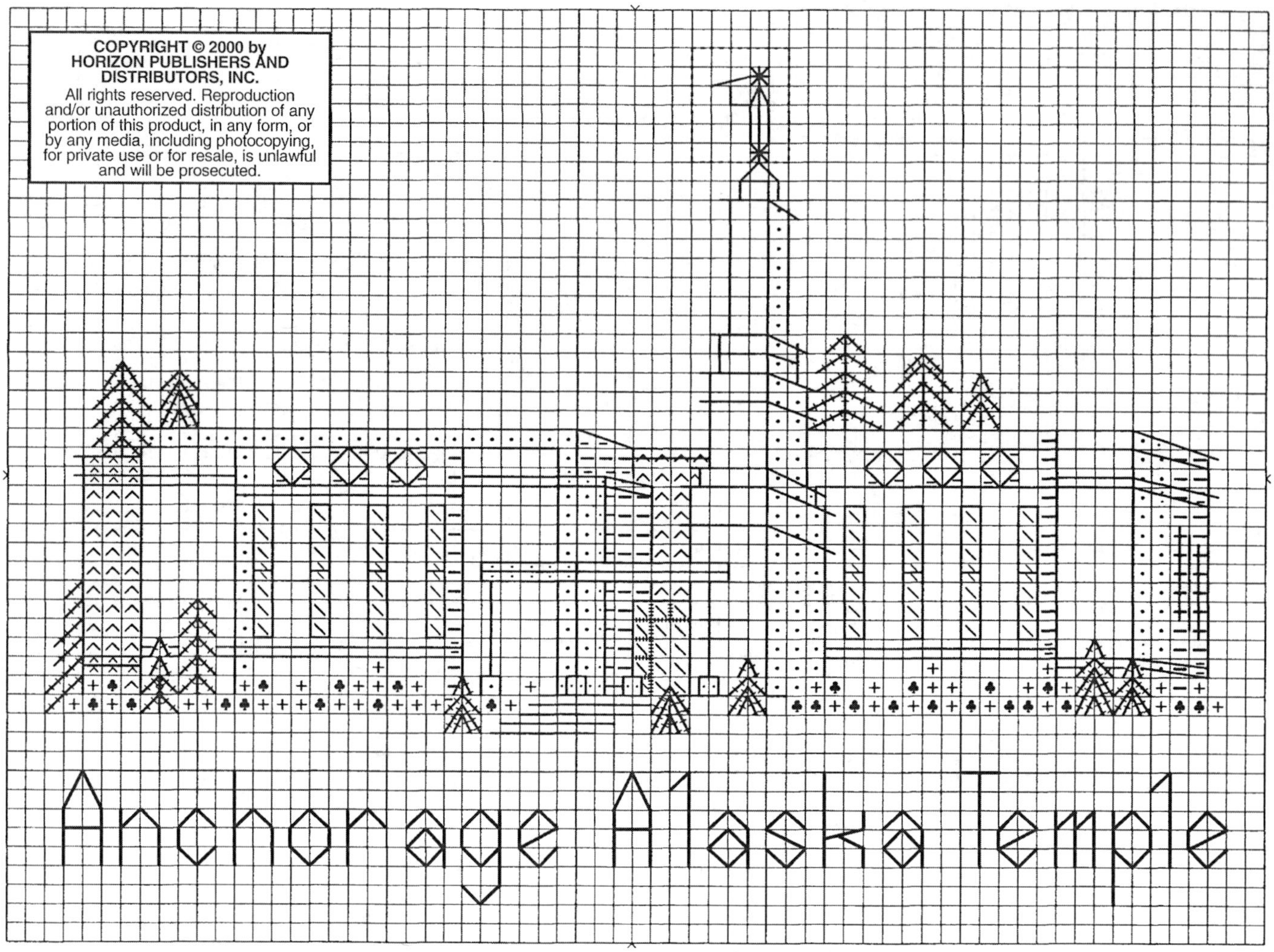

Design size: 62 x 35 squares; 62 x 44 with name of temple included.

Symbol	DMC	Anchor	JP Coats	Color Name	Description
□ (within pattern)	762	397	8510	pale gray	main body of temple
•	318	399	8511	light gray	light shadowing
—	317	401	8514	medium gray	medium shadowing
^	414	400	8512	dark gray	dark shadowing
\	775	128	7031	light blue	windows and glass door
+	368	214	6016	light pine green	shrubs
♣	367	217	6018	medium pine green	shrubs
—+—+—	319	1044	6021	dark pine green	backstitch evergreen trees
'''''''''''''''	762	397	8510	pale gray	backstitch lines in front door area
———	413	401	8999	dark gray	backstitch outline of temple
———	3820	307	2307	gold	backstitch Angel Moroni (within dashed lines)

Special Instructions

Before beginning to stitch this temple, be sure to read the *General Instructions* on pages 5-7 for information on partial stitches, the ledges, and the Angel Moroni.

DO NOT STITCH the dashed lines around the Angel Moroni. They are there to indicate that the angel and ball are to be backstitched with gold floss. The gold floss can be combined with a metallic floss or blending filament, if desired, to add a gold shine to the project.

This temple is located in Anchorage, Alaska. It was dedicated on January 9, 1999.

Colonia Juarez Chihuahua Mexico Temple Chart and Instructions

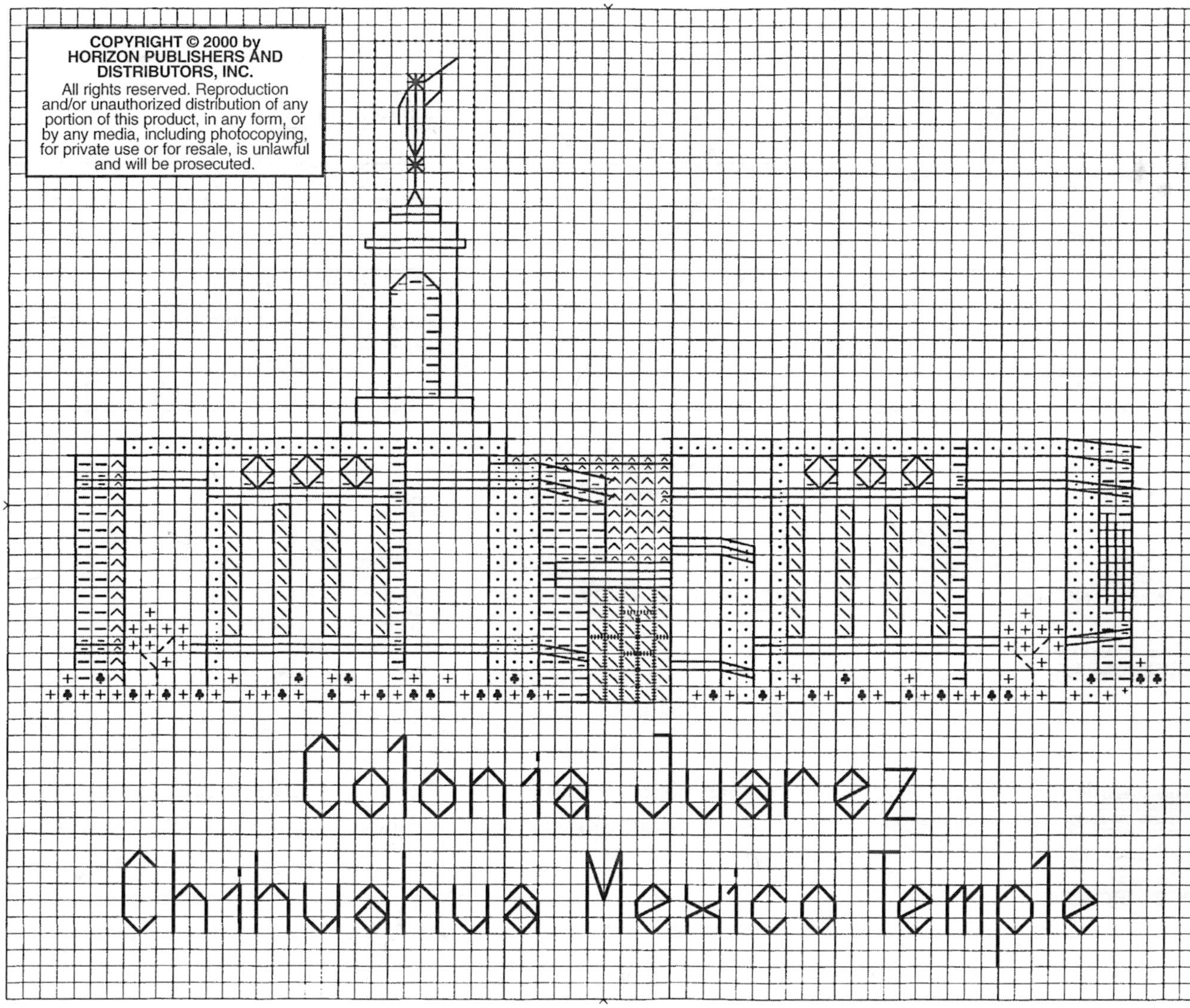

Design size: 66 x 40 squares; 66 x 49 with name of temple included.

Symbol	DMC	Anchor	JP Coats	Color Name	Description
□ (within pattern)	white	1	1001	white	main body of temple
•	762	397	8510	pale gray	light shadowing
—	318	399	8511	light gray	medium shadowing
^	414	400	8512	medium gray	darker shadowing
\	775	128	7031	light blue	windows and glass door
+	906	256	6256	light grass green	shrubs and leaves
♣	904	258	6267	medium grass green	shrubs and leaves
- - - -	801	359	5475	brown	backstitch tree trunks
············	762	397	8510	pale gray	backstitch lines in front door area
———	413	401	8999	dark gray	backstitch outline of temple
———	3820	307	2307	gold	backstitch Angel Moroni (within dashed lines)

Special Instructions

Before beginning to stitch this temple, be sure to read the *General Instructions* on pages 5-7 for information on partial stitches, the ledges, and the Angel Moroni.

DO NOT STITCH the dashed lines around the Angel Moroni. They are there to indicate that the angel and ball are to be backstitched with gold floss. The gold floss can be combined with a metallic floss or blending filament, if desired, to add a gold shine to the project.

This temple is located in Colonia Juarez, Chihuahua, Mexico. It was dedicated March 6, 1999.

Spokane Washington Temple Instructions

Symbol	DMC	Anchor	JP Coats	Color Name	Description
□ (within pattern)	white	1	1001	white	main body of temple
•	762	397	8510	pale gray	light shadowing
—	415	398	8398	light gray	medium shadowing
^	318	399	8511	medium gray	dark shadowing
\	775	128	7031	light blue	windows and glass door
+	368	214	6016	light pine green	shrubs
♣	367	217	6018	medium pine green	shrubs
┼┼┼	319	1044	6021	dark pine green	backstitch evergreen trees
'''''''''''''	762	397	8510	pale gray	backstitch lines in front door area
———	413	401	8999	deep gray	backstitch outline of temple
———	3820	307	2307	gold	backstitch Angel Moroni (within dashed lines)

Design size: 120 x 90 squares;
120 x 99 with name of temple included.

Special Instructions

Before beginning to stitch this temple, be sure to read the *General Instructions* on pages 5-7 for information on partial stitches, the ledges, and the Angel Moroni.

This temple is built of very light gray granite with flecks of darker gray scattered through the stone. If you wish to indicate this coloring, stitch the main color and shadings of the temple first. Then, using one strand at of a time of #762, #318 or #415, randomly stitch a full cross-stitch or the first diagonal stitch on top of the existing stitches.

The squares behind the window designs have been left unstitched. If you wish to indicate light shining through the windows, choose a color of light yellow, gold or peach floss. Stitch the windows with one strand of floss before backstitching the window designs.

When adapting this pattern to stitch another one of the temples built to this same basic design, be sure to read the *Instructions for Pattern Variations For Individual Temples*, pages 22-23, to decide on other possible color shadings, landscaping options and the direction for the Angel Moroni to face.

DO NOT STITCH the dashed lines around the Angel Moroni. They are there to indicate that the angel and ball are to be backstitched with gold floss. The gold floss can be combined with a metallic floss or blending filament, if desired, to add a gold shine to the project.

This view is looking at the front entrance of the temple. The name for the *Spokane Washington Temple* is included on this page. This pattern can be used for all 35 temples found listed on page 5, after changing the direction of the Angel Moroni, the stone colors and the landscape details. The names of other temples can be drafted on graph paper by using the alphabet and directions on page 24.

This temple is located in Spokane, Washington. It was dedicated on August 21, 1999.

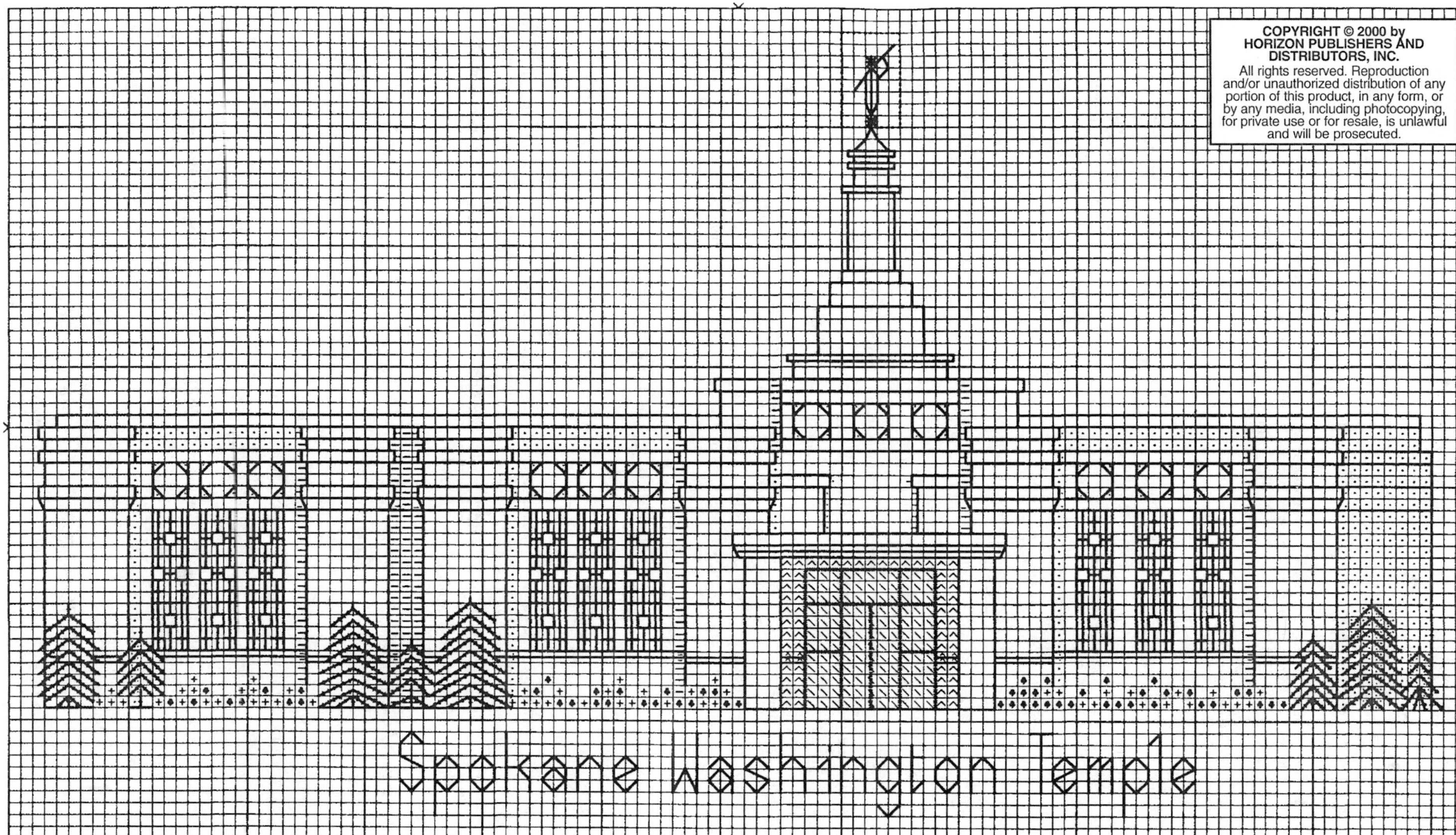
Spokane Washington Temple

Columbia South Carolina Temple Instructions

Symbol	DMC	Anchor	JP Coats	Color Name	Description of Area
empty square within pattern □	3865	2	1001	winter white	main body of temple
•	762	397	8510	pale gray	light shadows
–	318	399	8511	light gray	stone color variations[1]
×	523	859	6316	pale country green	stone color variations[1]
/	928	274	6005	light blue	stone color variations[1]
♡	3774	778	2336	light coral	stone color variations[1]
○	644	391	5831	light brown	stone color variations[1]
+	989	379	5379	light green	shrubs and tree leaves
♣	987	244	6258	medium green	shrubs and tree leaves
▬ ▬ ▬	433	358	5471	dark brown	backstitch tree trunks
▬▬▬	3820	307	3207	gold	backstitch Angel Moroni[2]
▬▬▬	413	401	8999	deep gray	backstitch outline of temple

[1] Although the general color of these temples is generally white, the marble in many of these temples sometimes has slight color striations spread through the stone. If you wish to indicate this marbling, stitch the main color and shadings of the temple first. Then, using just one strand of varied light colors as indicated in the above color key, randomly stitch a full cross-stitch or the first diagonal stitch on top of the existing stitches.

[2] DO NOT STITCH THE DOTTED LINE AROUND THE ANGEL MORONI. It indicates the area to be stitched in gold floss. You may combine one strand of metallic floss to two strands of gold in your needle. The squares for the angel's head and the ball upon which he stands are worked as a normal cross stitch (x), then adding a (+) directly on top of the (x) to create a rounded look.

Design Size 91 x 63 squares;
91 x 72 with name of temple included.

Special Instructions

This view is looking towards the Celestial Room side of the temple. The name for the *Columbia South Carolina Temple* is included on this page. This pattern can be used for all 35 temples found listed on page 5, after changing the direction of the Angel Moroni, the stone colors and the landscape details. The names of other temples can be drafted on graph paper by using the alphabet and directions on page 24.

Before beginning to stitch this temple, be sure to read the *General Instructions* on pages 5-7 for information on partial stitches, the ledges and the Angel Moroni.

The squares behind the window designs have been left unstitched. If you wish to indicate light shining through the windows, choose a color of light yellow, gold or peach floss. Stitch the windows with one strand of floss before backstitching around the window squares.

When adapting this pattern to stitch another temple built to the same basic design, be sure to read the *Instructions for Pattern Variations for Individual Temples* pages 22-23, to decide on other possible stone colors, landscaping options and the direction for the Angel Moroni to face.

This temple is located in Hopkins, just a few miles southeast of Columbia, South Carolina. It was dedicated on October 16, 1999 by President Gordon B. Hinckley.

Columbia South Carolina Temple

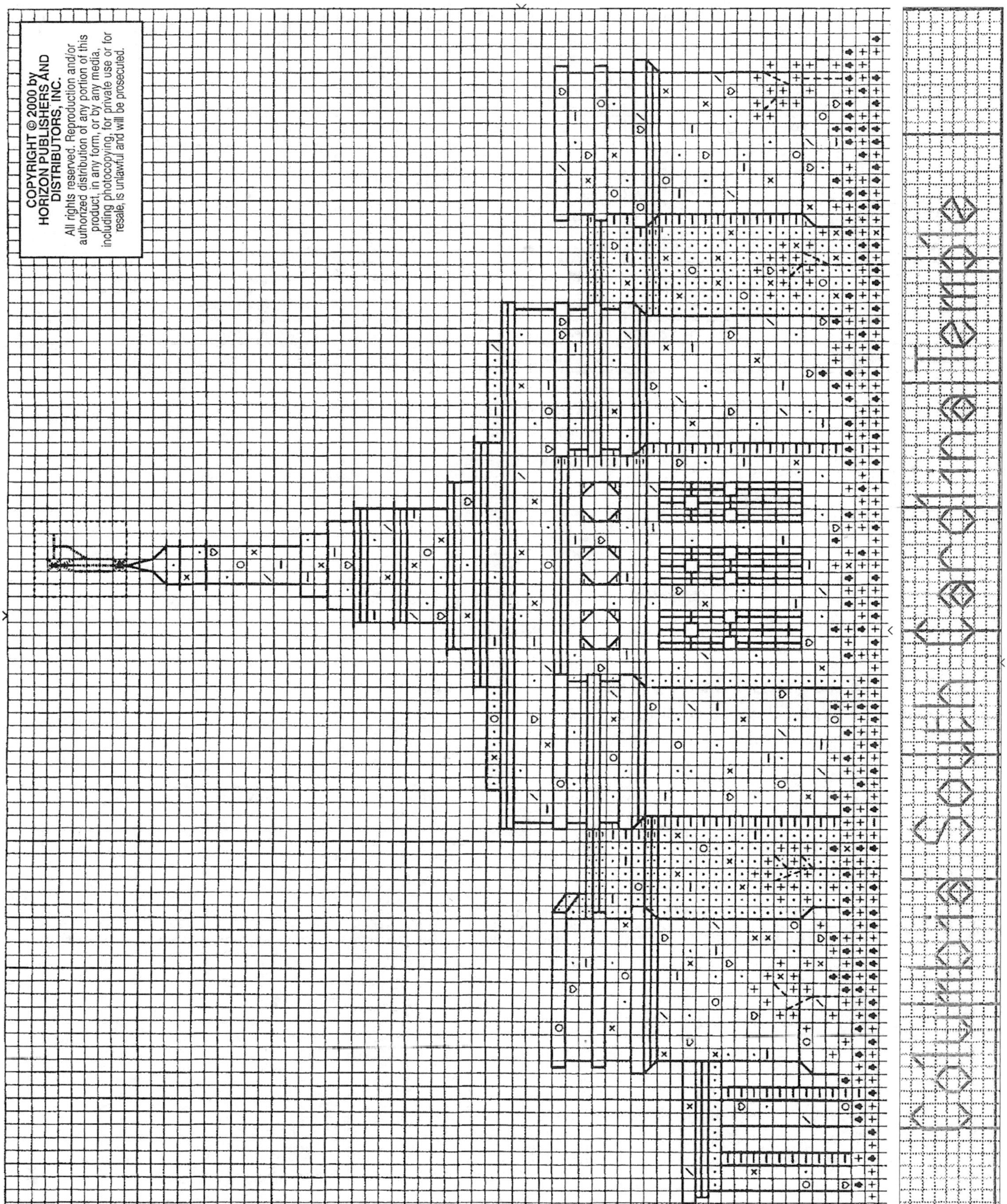

Raleigh North Carolina Temple Instructions

Symbol	DMC	Anchor	JP Coats	Color Name	Description
□ (within pattern)	3865	2	1001	winter white	main body of temple
•	712	387	8387	cream	light shadowing
▬	822	390	5933	pale beige	medium shadowing
^	644	391	5831	light beige	darker shadowing
▌	642	392	5832	beige	darkest shadowing
\	775	128	7031	light blue	windows and glass door
+	989	242	6266	light green	shrubs and leaves
♣	987	244	6258	medium green	shrubs and leaves
- - - - -	433	358	5471	brown	backstitch tree trunks
'''''''''''''''	3865	2	1001	winter white	backstitch lines in front door area
———	3371	382	5382	deep gray	backstitch outline of temple
———	3820	307	2307	gold	backstitch Angel Moroni (within dashed lines)

Design size: 108 x 58 squares;
108 x 67 with name of temple included.

Special Instructions

Before beginning to stitch this temple, be sure to read the *General Instructions* on pages 5-7 for information on partial stitches, the ledges, and the Angel Moroni.

The squares behind the window designs have been left unstitched. If you wish to indicate light shining through the windows, choose a color of light yellow, gold or peach floss. Stitch the windows with one strand of floss before backstitching the window designs.

When adapting this pattern to stitch another one of the temples built to this same basic design, be sure to read the *Instructions for Pattern Variations For Individual Temples*, pages 22-23, to decide on other possible color shadings, landscaping options and the direction for the Angel Moroni to face.

DO NOT STITCH the dashed lines around the Angel Moroni. They are there to indicate that the angel and ball are to be backstitched with gold floss. The gold floss can be combined with a metallic floss or blending filament, if desired, to add a gold shine to the project.

This temple is located in Raleigh, North Carolina. It was dedicated on December 18, 1999.

Raleigh North Carolina Temple

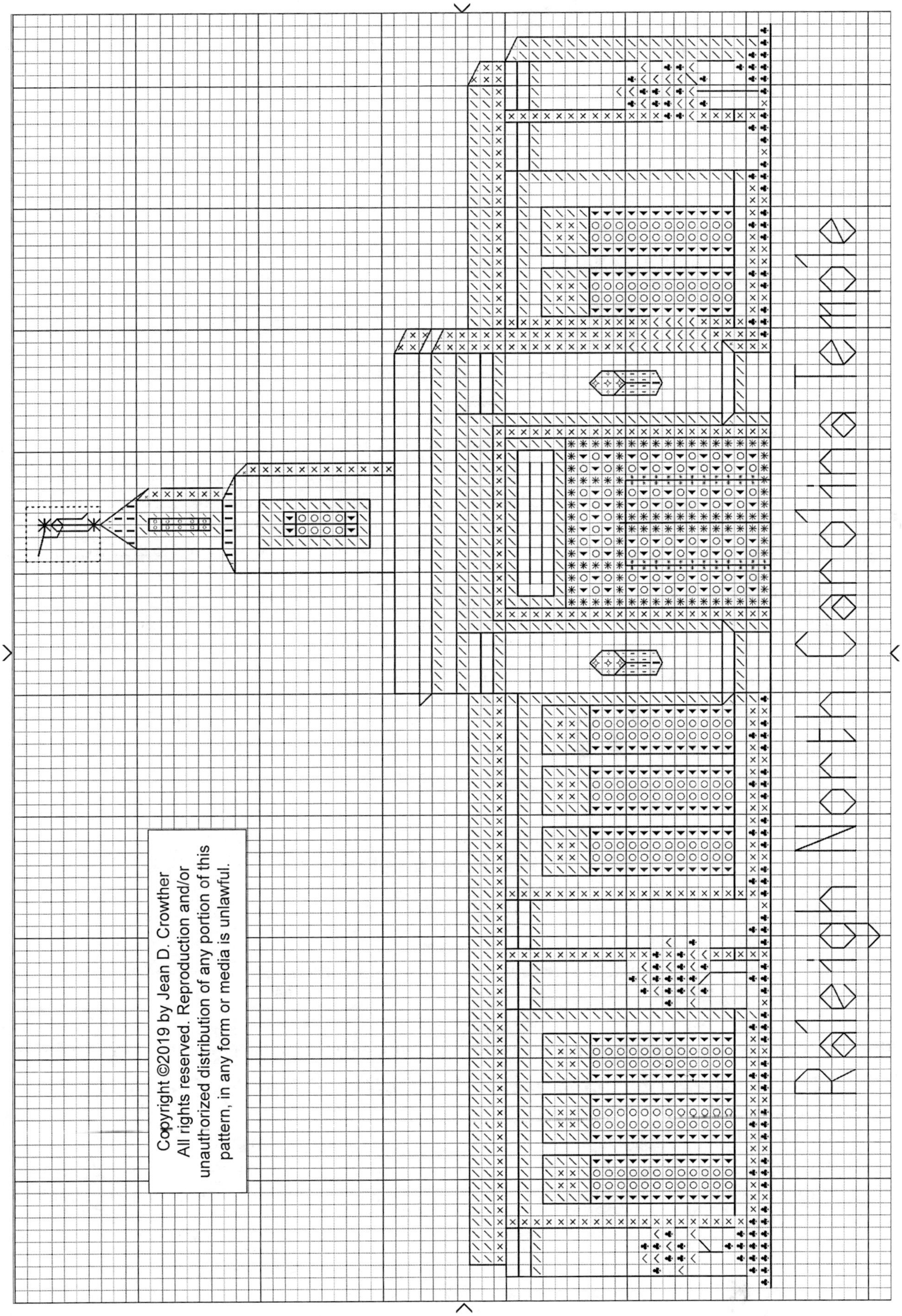

Raleigh North Carolina Temple Instructions

Symbol	DMC	Anchor	Color Name	Description of Area
empty square within pattern □	ecru	387	ecru	main body of temple
⁄	739	266	light beige	light shadows
×	437	262	medium beige	dark shadows
I	610	889	medium gray	light bases
✧	white	2	white	lamp bulbs
✳	434	310	golden brown	door frames
○	827	160	light blue	windows[1]
◀	3838	177	medium blue	windows[1]
^	912	209	light green	tree leaves
♣	910	230	medium green	tree leaves and bushes
▬	728	298	gold	backstitch Angel Moroni[2]
▬	869	375	dark beige	backstitch tree trunks and outline of temple

[1] The art glass windows and doors appear as blue shades in daylight. In the evening, the glass looks golden when the inside lights shine through. [The blue floss colors may be changed to two gold shades, possibly #728 and #744, but please stitch a small sample to check if the color combination is desirable to you. It will give the project a very different look.] The DMC Corporation makes a 6-strand Light Effects Floss in metallic and pastel colors. Adding one strand of Light Effects Floss to the two strands of floss in some random stitches will add a lovely shine to the windows.

[2] DO NOT STITCH THE DOTTED LINE AROUND THE ANGEL MORONI. It indicates the area to be stitched in gold floss. One strand of a beige floss may added to the two strands of floss in the needle to make the angel more distinct. Also, one strand of metallic or Light Effects Floss may also added. The squares for the angel's head and the ball upon which he stands are worked as a normal cross stitch (x), then adding a (+) directly on top of the (x) to create a rounded look.

This view is looking from the left side of the temple. The name for the *Palmyra New York Temple* is included on this page. This pattern can be used for all 35 temples found listed on page 5, after changing the direction of the Angel Moroni, the stone colors and the landscape details. The names of other temples can be drafted on graph paper by using the alphabet and directions on page 24.

Design Size 104 x 60 squares;
104 x 69 with name of temple included.

Special Instructions

Before beginning to stitch this temple, be sure to read the General Instructions on pages 5-7 for information on partial stitches and the Angel Moroni.

This pattern can also be used to stitch the following temples which have also been renovated to this design:

Baton Rouge Louisiana, Columbus Ohio and ***Memphis Tennessee.***

When adapting this pattern to stitch one of the other ones, be sure to read the Instruction for Pattern Variations for Individual Temples, pages 22-23, to decide on other possible color shadings, landscaping options and the direction for the Angel Moroni to face. Consulting the Church website or other photos of the chosen temples found on the Internet will aid in these decisions.

This temple is located in Apex, North Carolina, slightly west of Raleigh.
It was originally dedicated on December 18, 1999 by President Gordon B. Hinckley.
On January 7, 2018, it was closed for exterior and interior renovation.
It was re-dedicated on October 13, 2019 by President M. Russell Ballard.

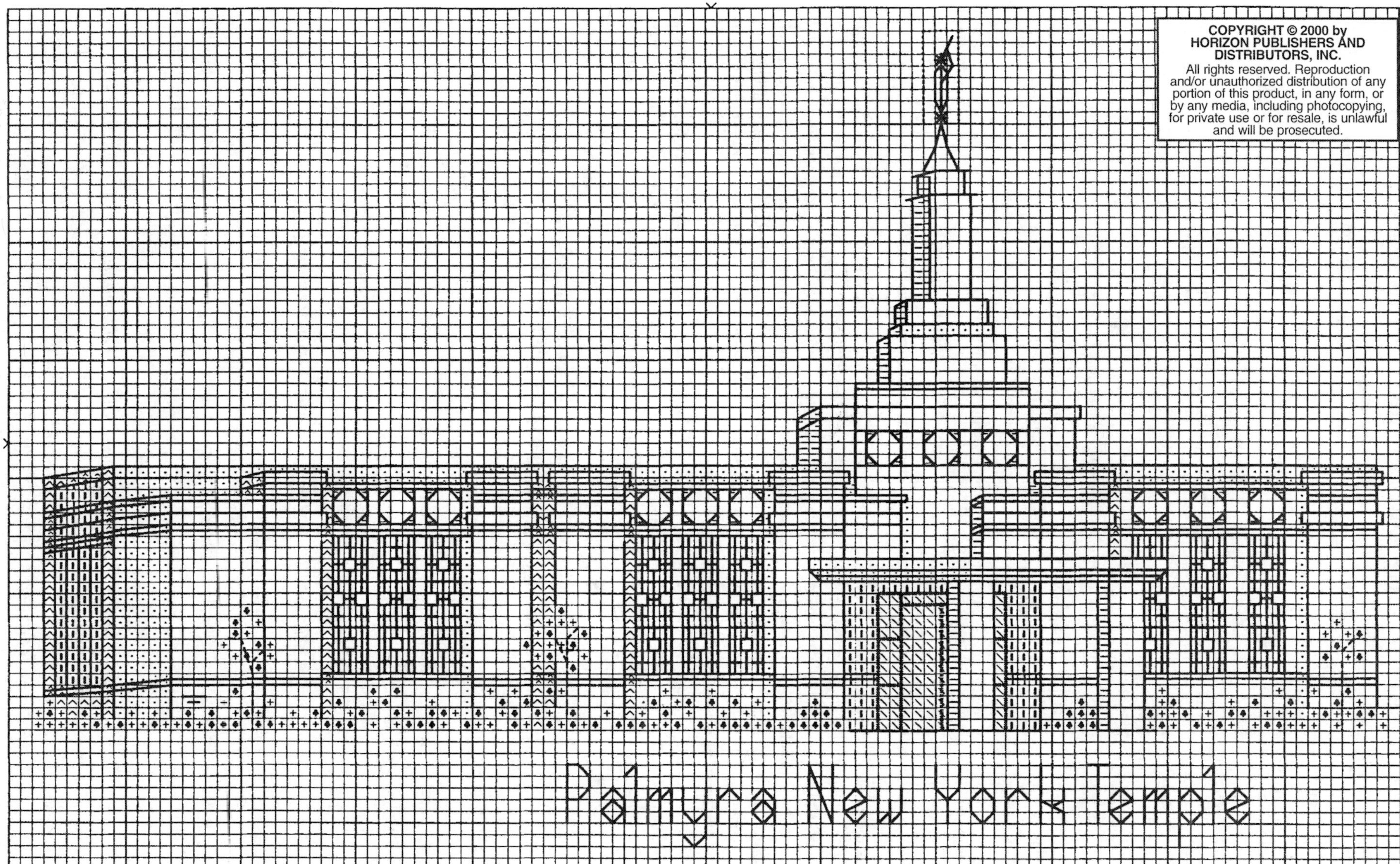
COPYRIGHT © 2000 by
HORIZON PUBLISHERS AND
DISTRIBUTORS, INC.
All rights reserved. Reproduction and/or unauthorized distribution of any portion of this product, in any form, or by any media, including photocopying, for private use or for resale, is unlawful and will be prosecuted.
Palmyra New York Temple

Oklahoma City Oklahoma Temple Instructions

Symbol	DMC	Anchor	Color Name	Description of Area
empty square within pattern □	white	1	white	main body of temple
/	3072	397	light gray	light shadows
×	647	400	medium gray	medium shadows
◀	317	398	dark gray	roof of tower
○	341	117	blue	windows and door glass[1]
^	912	209	medium green	tree leaves
♣	907	211	dark green	tree leaves and bushes
◆	781	308	bronze	door and window frames
◆◆◆	433	358	brown	backstitch tree trunks
▬ ▬ ▬	781	308	bronze	backstitch door frames
▬▬▬	725	305	gold	backstitch Angel Moroni[2]
▬▬▬	413	401	deep gray	backstitch outline of temple

[1] In photographs taken at different times of the day, the art glass in the windows and doors appears as different colors. During daylight hours the glass reflects shades of blue. At night, when lit from within, the glass glows in shades of light gold. You may stitch the windows in solid blue (as indicated in the color key) or choose to use a shade of light gold floss, such as DMC #728 or Anchor #302. To more closely simulate the art glass, a few shades of either blues or golds can be chosen. Then one strand of two different colors can be combined in the needle and random cross stitches can be scattered throughout the window areas. The DMC Corporation makes a 6-strand Light Effects Floss in metallic and pastel colors. Adding one strand to the two strands of flow in the needle of a shade of Light Effects Floss will add a lovely shine to the windows.
[2] DO NOT STITCH THE DOTTED LING AROUND THE ANGEL MORONI. It indicates the area to be stitched in gold floss. You may combine one strand of metallic or Light Effects Floss to two strands of gold in your needle. The squares for the angel's head and the ball upon which he stands are worked as a normal cross stitch (x), then adding a (+) directly on top of the (x) to create a rounded look.

Design Size 108 x 59 squares;
108 x 68 with name of temple included.

Special Instructions

Before beginning to stitch this temple, be sure to read the General Instructions on pages 5-7 for information on partial stitches and the Angel Moroni.

There were only two temples built with the original design flip-flopped and reversed 180°:

Oklahoma City and ***Asunción Paraguay.***

They both were renovated and the exterior of the Oklahoma City was updated as indicated in the pattern. The Paraguay temple exterior remained as originally designed. The Paraguay temple can be stitched using the Columbia South Carolina Temple pattern on page 15. It will be necessary to remove the porch portion on the left side of the chart, flip it 180° and add it at the same level on the right side of the pattern. Replace the Angel Moroni with the #D Angel on page 22.

This temple is located in Yukon, a suburb of Oklahoma City, Oklahoma.
It was originally dedicated on July 30, 2000 by President James E. Faust.
It was closed in 2017 for approximately two years for an extensive renovation.
It was rededicated on May 19, 2019 by President Henry B. Eyring.

Oklahoma City Oklahoma Temple

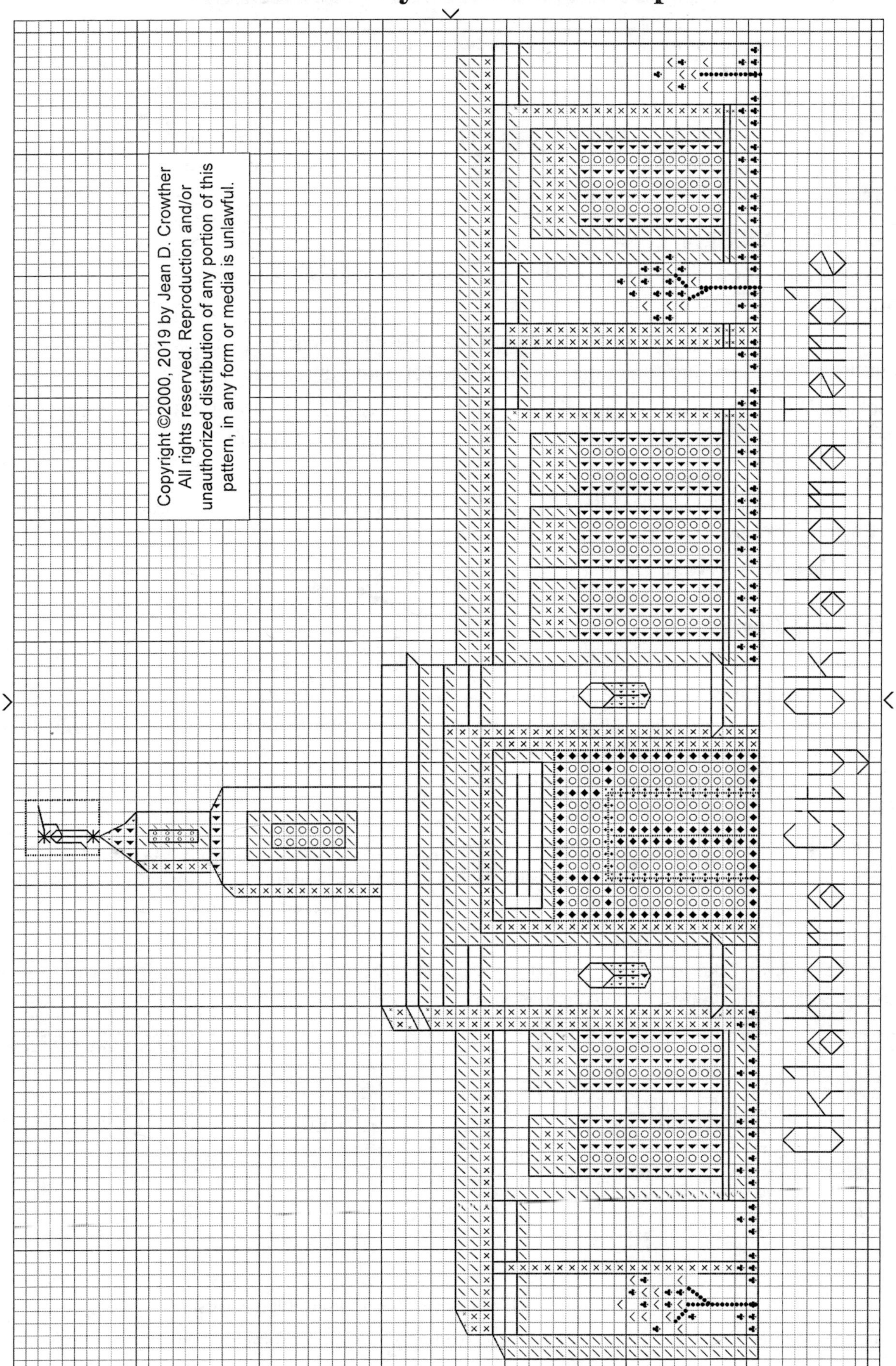

Instructions For Pattern Variations For Individual Temples

Variations of Stone Colors

The designs in this book have been charted with different color schemes utilizing various shades of floss to capture the color variations ranging from white marble to gray granite of stone used for the temples. When stitching a temple consider the following color possibilities:

1. The Palmyra New York Temple, page 18, has a color scheme of white marble with gray shadowing.
2. The Raleigh North Carolina Temple, page 16, has been designed in a white marble with rich cream shadowing.
3. The Columbus Ohio Tempe, page 14, was built out of a white marble that has colored striations through the stone. There are directions on that page for using that technique.
4. The Spokane Washington Temple, page 12, is built from a very light gray granite with light flecks of grey, but it gives a generally white appearance. There are directions on that page for that type of stone.
5. The Anchorage Alaska Temple, page 10, is designed with a pale gray base color and slightly darker shadowing for temples built from darker gray granite.

The Monticello Utah Temple, page 9, has it's own color scheme of very light variegated cream cast stone.

Variations of the Front Doors

It seems that most of these newer temples have a glass door surrounded by small windows. Most of the former temples have doors of bronze or dark wood. The Oklahoma City Oklahoma Temple, page 20, has been designed with a wooden door color. That variation may be used for a temple with solid doors by changing the light blue of the actual door to the golden brown color as indicated on page 20. Remember to also change the light backstitch around the door to the main backstitch color.

Variations of the Angel Moroni

The Angel Moroni is placed on the top of each temple, always facing east, no matter which way the temple itself faces. Each temple is built to take the best advantage of the available land upon which it is situated so the entrance might face in any direction.

The angle of the horn and the angel's extended arms are determined by the direction from which it is viewed. Following are possible views of the Angel Moroni:

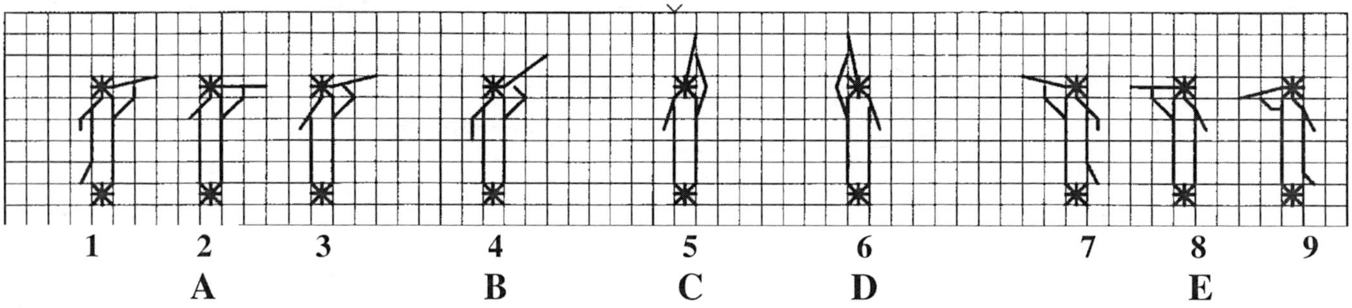

A: Numbers 1, 2 and 3: Temples generally facing North

B: Number 4: Temples facing Southeast

C: Number 5: Temples facing East

D: Number 6: Temples facing West

E: Numbers 7, 8 and 9: Temples generally facing South

Variations of Landscaping Details

The landscaping in the charts for the temples in this book has reflected the smaller bushes and trees in place as the temples have been dedicated and this book has been published. The designer has added plants to the obvious areas and where planting boxes were built during construction. Local stitchers may wish to change the pattern to better reflect the size and shape of the bushes and trees at the time the pattern is stitched.

Because of the different climates of the world, a stitcher adapting the Raleigh North Carolina Temple pattern to stitch one of the Mexico temples might substitute palm trees in place of the smaller trees in the design. Someone adapting the Spokane Temple pattern for the Memphis Tennessee Temple will change the evergreen trees across the front to dogwood and magnolia trees.

Following are patterns for several trees and bushes which can be used to individualize the temple design you stitch. The size of the trees can be easily changed by adding more length to the trunk or more squares at the top. If you wish to create a flowering bush or tree, randomly add a few squares of the desired color in empty squares or in place of a green symbol.

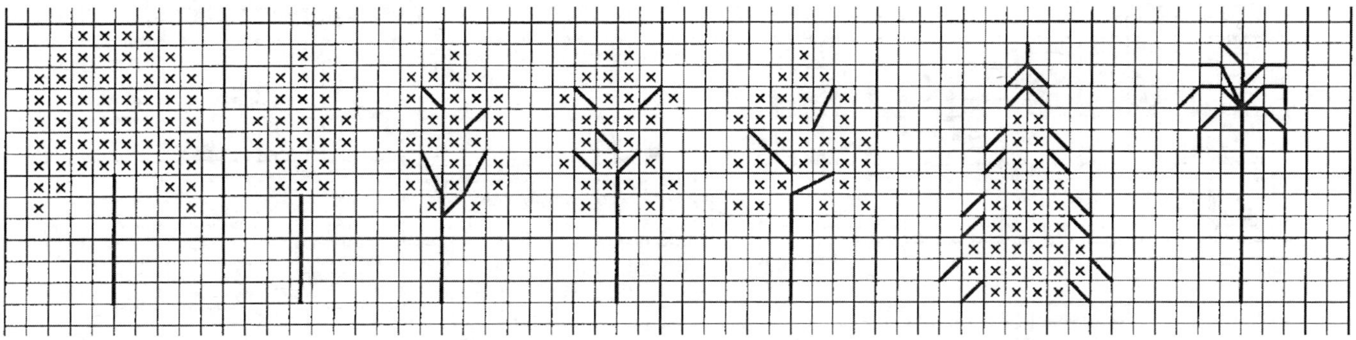

A B C

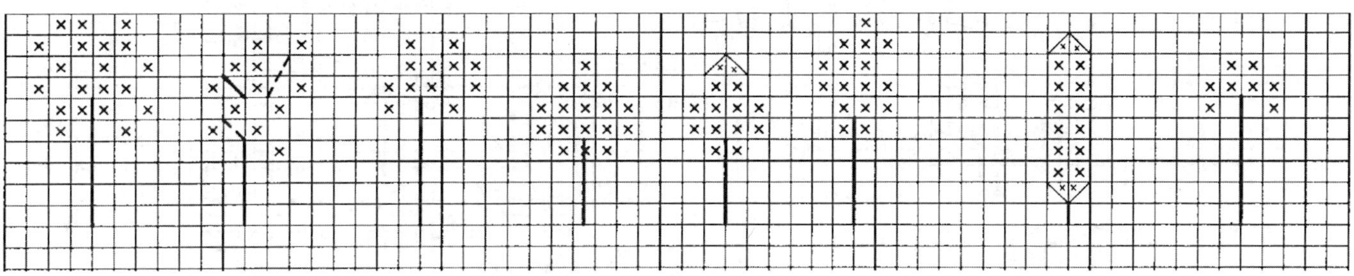

D E F

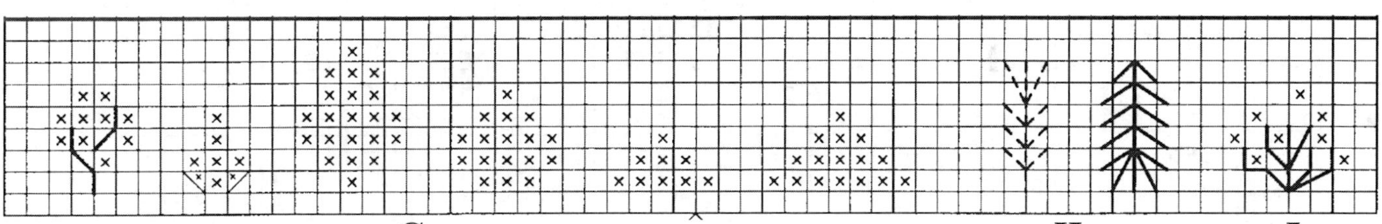

G H I

A: Large trees
B: Evergreen tree
C: Palm tree
D: Medium-height trees
E: Popular or Cypress tree
F: Smaller palm tree
G: Bushes
H: Small evergreen trees
I: Flowering bush (add color where desired)

Alphabet Instructions and Chart

The small alphabet is used for the names of the temples charted in this book. A stitcher creating another temple pattern should use the small alphabet for the name of the temple. It should also be used to add names to personalize the project. The large alphabet can be used as is, or color can be added in the empty squares. When designing additional words, allow a single square between letters and three squares between words. Center each line, using the centering arrow of the temple as the beginning reference. Be sure to add the extra line count into the height of the total design-size calculations of the temple before beginning to stitch.